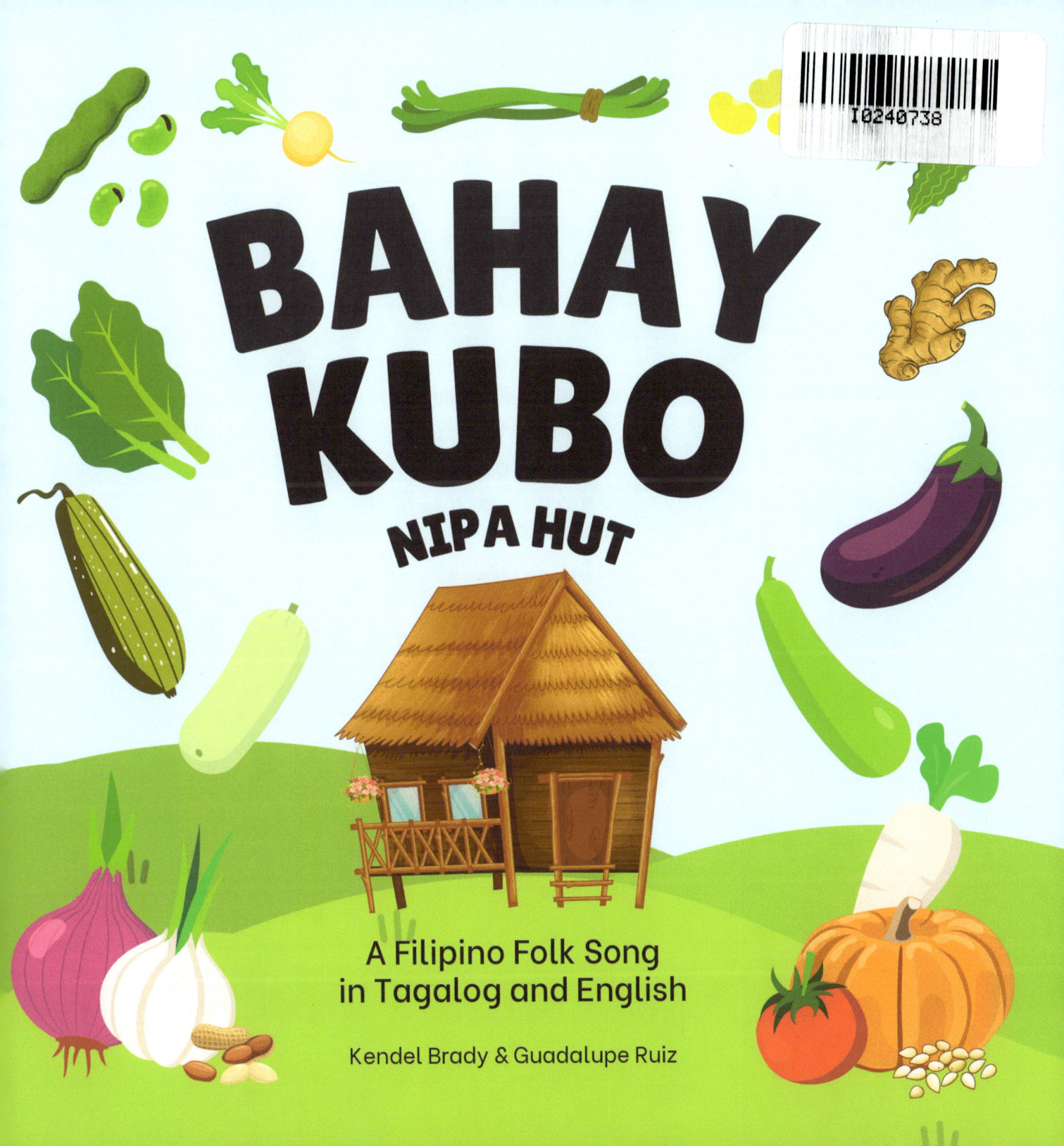

This book is dedicated to YOU,
a steward of Earth. May you discover the
magic that is in you and in nature.
May we build a legacy of love and
sustainability by sharing the simple joy of
growing and eating food from the land.

Published by Educating Abroad, LLC
Guadalupe Ruiz and Kendel Brady © 2025

No portion of this publication may be reproduced or transmitted in any form or by any means, electronic or mechanical, including, but not limited to, audio recordings, facsimiles, photocopying, or information storage and retrieval systems without explicit written permission from the author or publisher.

Download our Free Bahay Kubo Companion Activities!

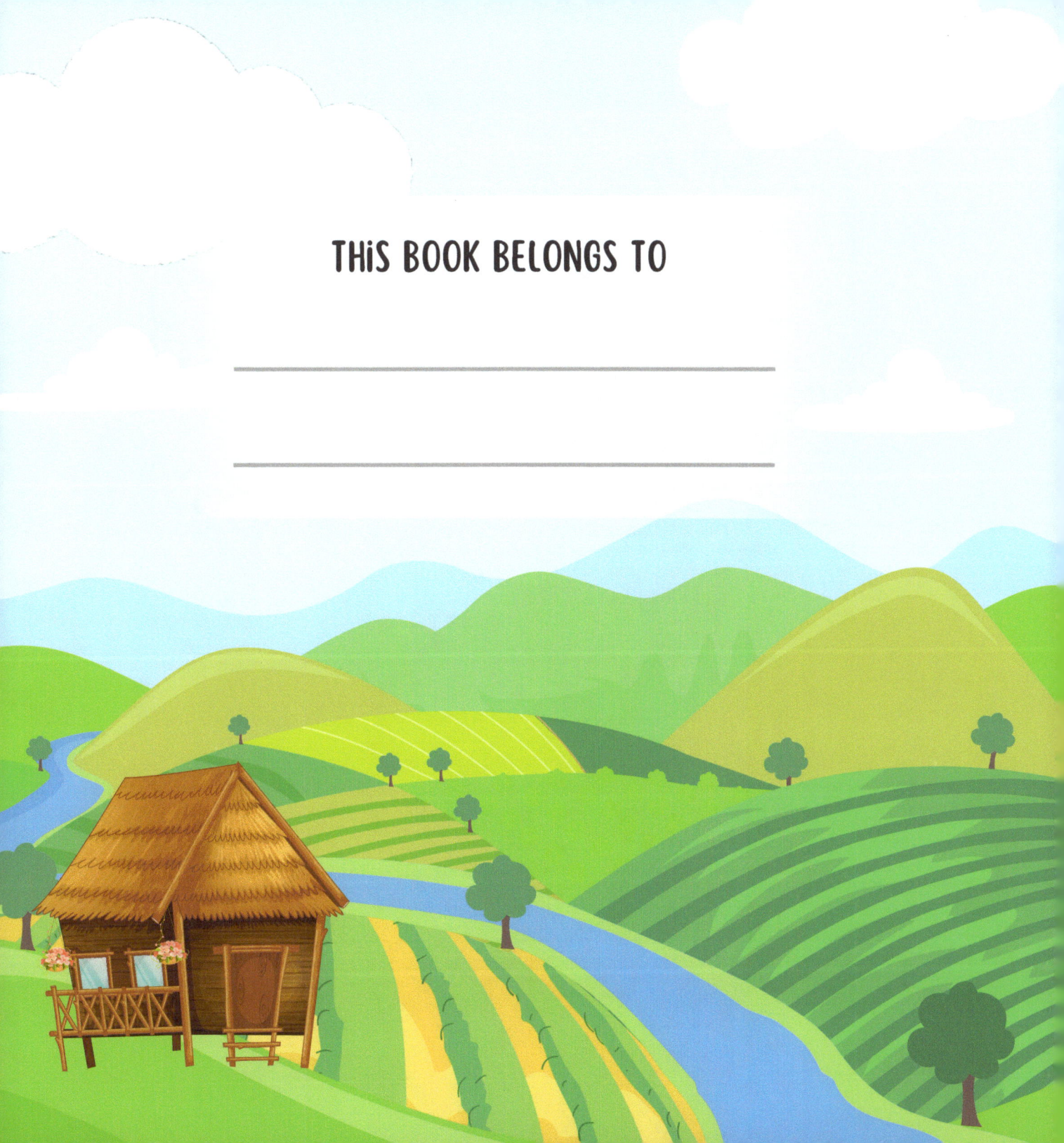

ang halaman doon ay sari-sari.

the plants there are varied.

at talong
and eggplant

sitaw
long beans

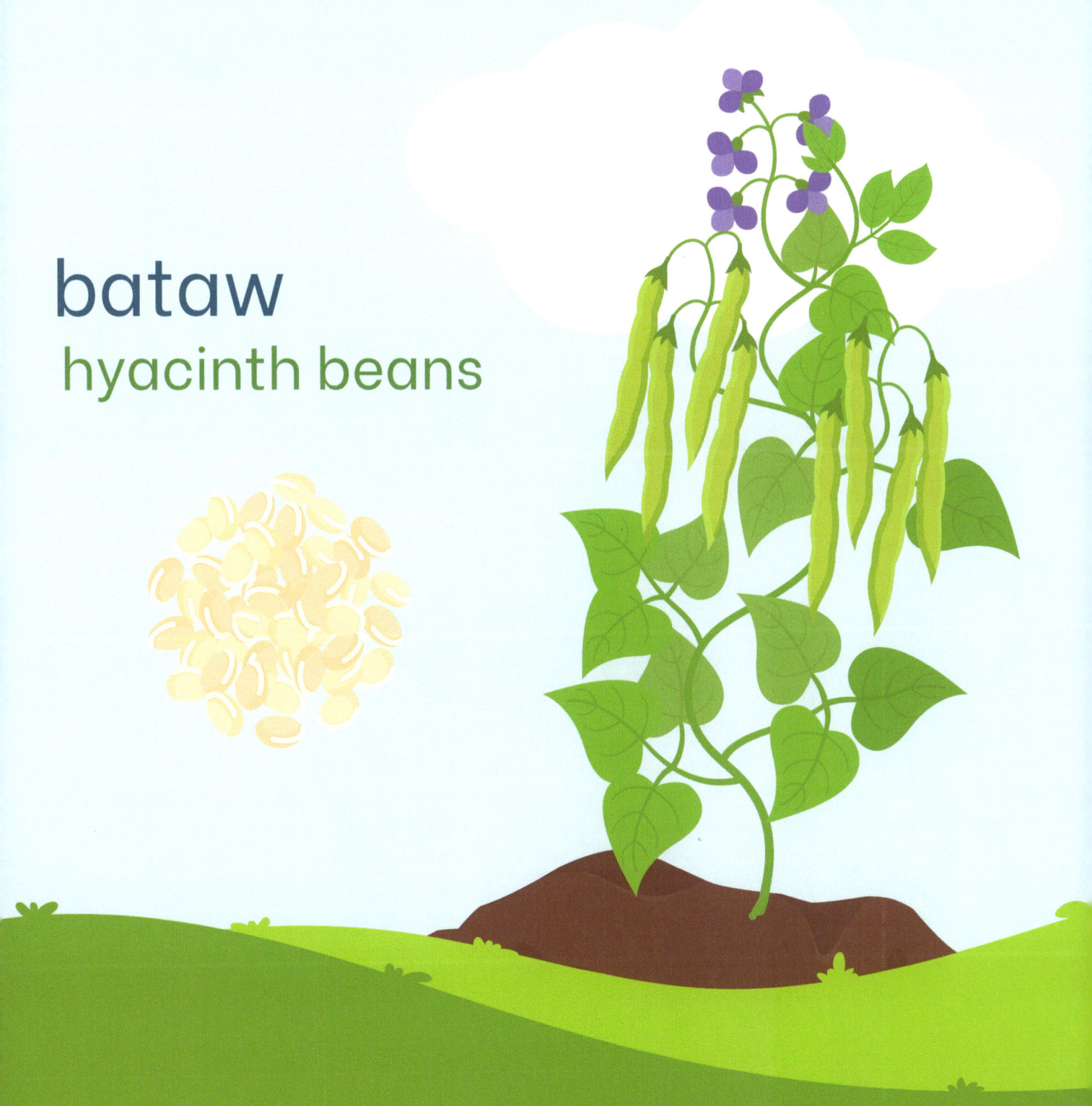

patani
lima beans

upo't
bottle gourd and

at saka mayroon pang **labanos**

and there is also **radish**

mustasa
mustard greens

at luya
and ginger

sa paligid-ligid ay puno ng **linga**.

all around are **sesame** plants.

Bahay Kubo
Folk song from the Philippines

Bahay Kubo

Folk song from the Philippines

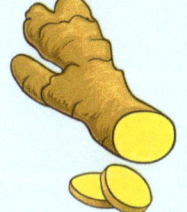

Filipino

Bahay kubo, kahit munti,
ang halaman doon,
ay sari sari.

Singkamas at talong,
sigarilyas at mani,
sitaw, bataw,
patani.

Kundol, patola,
upo't, kalabasa,
at saka mayroon pang
labanos, mustasa.

Sibuyas, kamatis,
bawang at luya,
sa paligid-ligid
ay puno ng linga.

English

Nipa hut, though small,
the plants there
are varied.

Turnip and eggplant,
winged bean and peanut,
long bean, hyacinth bean,
lima bean.

Winter melon, sponge gourd,
bottle gourd and pumpkin,
and there is also
radish, mustard greens.

Onion, tomato,
garlic, and ginger,
all around
are sesame plants.

Itugma ang pagkain sa pangalan nito!

Singkamas (Turnip)

Talong (Eggplant)

Sigarilyas (Winged Beans)

Mani (Peanuts)

Sitaw (Long Beans)

Bataw (Hyacinth Beans)

Patani (Lima Beans)

Kundol (Winter Melon)

Patola (Sponge Gourd)

Match the food to its name!

Upo (Bottle Gourd)

Kalabasa (Pumpkin)

Labanos (Radish)

Mustasa (Mustard Greens)

Sibuyas (Onion)

Kamatis (Tomatoes)

Bawang (Garlic)

Luya (Ginger)

Linga (Sesame)

ABOUT THE AUTHORS

Guada is a Filipino author and special education teacher who grew up in Cebu City, Philippines. She spent her summers in the province, riding carabaos, foraging food, and bathing in the rivers. She loves sharing stories about the simplicity of the traditional Filipino culture and way of life.

www.thecleverpinoy.com

Kendel is an American author and educator who cherishes joyful childhood memories spent in nature and gardening alongside her grandparents. Currently, she resides in Bohol, Philippines, where she enjoys an abundant backyard garden.
www.kendelbrady.com

Guada and Kendel hope readers of all ages will sing this book with delight as they learn to identify different plants and take part in the preservation of Filipino culture and language.

Free Printable Memory Game

Continue learning! This book has a free printable memory card game designed to reinforce Tagalog and English vocabulary through hands-on learning.

Download the Free Companion Activities!
www.kendelbrady.com

If your child enjoyed this book, you may also love:

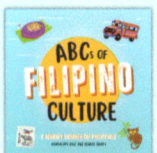

ABCs of Filipino Culture
An alphabet picture book that introduces Filipino culture through letters, words, and conversation.

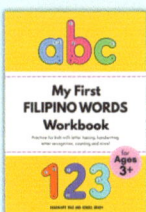

My First Filipino Words Workbook
A hands-on activity book for preschool and kindergarten learners that builds early literacy, handwriting, and number recognition using Filipino cultural vocabulary.

Baybayin Workbook
A beginner-friendly workbook for teens and adults interested in learning the ancient Philippine writing system.